DRAMATIC WORKS
AND
DIALOGUES

From the same publishers

Samuel Beckett

Novels

Dream of Fair to Middling Women (1932)
Murphy (1938)
Watt (1945)
First Love (1945)
Mercier and Camier (1946)
Molloy (1951)*
Malone Dies (1951)*

The Unnamable (1953) *
How It Is (1961)
Company (1980)**
Ill Seen Ill Said (1981)**
Worstward Ho (1983)**
* published together as the Trilogy
** published together as Nohow On

Short Prose

More Pricks than Kicks (1934)
Collected Short Prose (in preparation)
Beckett Shorts (see below)

Poetry

Collected Poems (1930-1978)
Anthology of Mexican Poetry
(translations)

Criticism
Proust & Three Dialogues with Georges Duthuit (1931,1949)
Disjecta (1929-1967)

Beckett Shorts (A collection of 12 short volumes to commemorate the writer's death in 1989)
1. Texts for Nothing (1947-52)
2. Dramatic Works and Dialogues (1938-67)
3. All Strange Away (1963)
4. Worstward Ho (1983)
5. Six Residua (1957-72)
6. For to End Yet Again (1960-75)

7. The Old Tune (1962)
8. First Love (1945)
9. As the Story Was Told
10. Three Novellas (1945-6)
11. Stirrings Still (1986-9)
12. Selected Poems (1930-85)

DRAMATIC WORKS
AND
DIALOGUES

Samuel Beckett

JOHN CALDER
LONDON

This edition first published 1999 as a collection in Great Britain by
John Calder Publishers
London

Human Wishes first published in Disjecta by John Calder
(Publishers) Ltd 1983.
Come and Go first published by Calder and Boyars 1967
Three Dialogues with George Duthuit first published in Transition
1949, subsequently by John Calder (Publishers) Ltd in 1965,
reprinted by Calder and Boyars Ltd 1970.

British Library Cataloguing in Publication Data
A catalogue record for this title is available from the British
Library

Printed in Canada by Webcom Ltd

Human Wishes

A room in Bolt Court. Wednesday, April 14th, 1781. Evening.

Mrs Williams *(meditating)*.
Mrs Desmoulins *(knitting)*.
Miss Carmichael *(reading)*.
The cat Hodge *(sleeping — if possible)*.

Mrs D.   He is late.

Silence.

Mrs D.   God grant all is well.

Silence.

Mrs D.   Puss puss puss puss puss.

Silence.

Mrs W.   What are you reading, young woman?

Miss C.   A book, Madam.

Mrs W.   Ha!

Silence.

Mrs D.   Hodge is a very fine cat, a very fine cat indeed.

Silence.

Mrs D.   For his age, an uncommonly fine cat in all respects.
When Hodge was a younger cat, I well remember —

Mrs W.   You are knotting, Madam, I perceive.

Mrs D.   That is so, Madam.

Mrs W.   What?

5

Mrs D.   I am knotting, my dear Madam, a mitten.

Mrs W.   Ha!

Mrs D.   The second of a pair.

Silence.

Mrs W.   What book, young woman?

Silence.

Mrs W.   *(loudly).* I say, WHAT BOOK?

Miss C.   Upon my soul, Madam, your perceptions are very fine, very fine indeed, uncommonly fine in all respects.

Mrs W.   I may be old, I may be blind, halt and maim, I may be dying of a pituitous defluxion, but my hearing is unimpaired.

Miss C.   And your colloquial powers.

Mrs D.   Dying of a what, my dear Madam?

Mrs W.   And while I continue to live, or rather to respire, I hope I shall never submit to be insulted by sluts, slovens, upstarts, parasites and intruders.

Mrs D.   Come, come, my dear lady.

Mrs W.   Knot on, Madam, knot on, or endeavour to talk like a sensible woman.

Mrs D.   You wish to provoke me, Madam, but I am not provoked. The peevishness of decay is not provoking.

Miss C.   Insupportable hag.

Mrs D.   *(rising).* That is not the language of a gentlewoman, Miss Carmichael.

Miss C.   *(rising).* I have not the advantage, Madam, of being the relict of a writing-master.

Mrs W.   *(striking the floor with her stick).* Be seated; and let your scurrility be the recumbent scurrility of polite society.

Miss C.   Nor the daughter of a Welsh mechanic.

Mrs D.   Of whom you are the relict, Miss Carmichael, or of how many, I prefer not to enquire.

Mrs W.   Were I not loath, Madam, to abase myself to your syntax, I could add: or of whom the daughter, or of how many.

Miss C.   *(laughs heartily, sits down and resumes her book).*

Mrs W.   Is the jest yours, Madam, or it is mine?

Mrs D.   To be called a loose woman would not move me to mirth, for my part, I believe. *(Sits down).*

Mrs W.   And to be called the daughter of a loose woman, would that move you to mirth, Madam, for your part, do you suppose?

Mrs D.   It would not, Madam, I believe.

Mrs W.   But what would move you, Madam, to mirth, do you suppose, for your part?

Mrs D.   To mirth, Madam, for my part, I am with difficulty moved, I believe.

Silence.

Mrs W.   Madam, for mirth, for my part,
         I never had the heart;
         Madam, for my part, to mirth
         I have not been moved since birth.

Silence.

Mrs W.   Please to take it down. I repeat. *(Repeats).*

Silence.

Mrs W.   Is it down?

Miss C.   It is, Madam. In what will not dry black and what was never white.

Mrs W.   Give it to me here in my hand.

Miss C.   *(rises, takes a blank sheet off the table, hands it to Mrs. W. and returns to her seat).*

7

Mrs W.   *(fingering the sheet tenderly)*. I did not hear the scratch of the quill.

Miss C.   I write very quiet.

Mrs W.   I do not feel the trace of the ink.

Miss C.   I write very fine. Very quiet, I write, and very fine.

Silence.

Mrs W.   Mrs Desmoulins.

Mrs D.   Madam.

Mrs W.   You have ceased to knot, I perceive.

Mrs D.   That is so, Madam.

Silence.

Mrs W.   Mrs Desmoulins.

Mrs D.   What is it, Madam?

Mrs W.   You say you are not merry. Very well. But who is merry in this house? You would not call me merry, Madam, I suppose?

Mrs D.   No, Madam, you are not what I would call merry.

Mrs W.   And Frank, Madam, would you call Frank merry?

Mrs D.   No, Madam, I would not.

Miss C.   Except when drunk.

Mrs D.   The gross hilarity of ebriety is not merriment, Miss Carmichael, to my mind.

Mrs W.   And Levett, Madam, would you call Levett merry?

Mrs D.   I would not call Levett anything, Madam.

Miss C.   Not even when drunk.

Mrs W.   And poor Poll here, Madam, is poor Poll here what you would call merry?

Mrs D.   She was taken into the house to be merry.

Mrs W. I do not ask why she was taken into the house. I ask is she merry or is she not merry.

Miss C. I was merry once, I think.

Mrs W. *(loudly)*. What is it to me, Miss, that you were merry once? Are you merry, or are you not merry, NOW?

Mrs D. She was taken in to enliven the house. I do not feel myself enlivened, for my part.

Mrs W. What you feel, Madam, and what you do not feel, is of little consequence.

Mrs D. I am aware of that, Madam.

Mrs W. I am not merry, you are not merry, Frank is not merry —

Miss C. Except when drunk.

Mrs W. Silence! Levett is not merry. Who remains?

Miss C. The cat.

Mrs W. *(striking the floor with her stick)*. Silence!

Silence.

Mrs W. The cat does *not* remain. The cat does not enter into the question. The cat *cannot* be merry.

Silence.

Mrs W. I ask, who remains?

Silence.

Mrs W. *(loudly)*. I ask, who remains, who might be merry?

Mrs D. Who was taken into the house to be merry.

Mrs W. *(striking the floor with her stick)*. Silence!

Silence.

Mrs W. I ask, who remains who might be merry, and I answer *(pointing her stick at Miss Carmichael)*, *she* remains.

Silence.

9

Mrs W.   Is she merry?

Silence.

Mrs W.   *(at the top of her voice).* IS SHE MERRY?

Miss C.   *(softly).* She is not.

Silence.

Mrs W.   *(softly).* Nobody in this house is merry.

Mrs D.   I hope you are satisfied, Madam.

Silence.

Miss C.   And the doctor, is the doctor. . . .

Silence.

Mrs D.   He is late.

Silence.

Mrs D.   God grant all is well.

Enter LEVETT, slightly, respectably, even reluctantly drunk, in great coat and hat, which he does not remove, carrying a small black bag. He advances unsteadily into the room & stands peering at the company. Ignored ostentatiously by Mrs D. (knitting), Miss Carmichael (reading), Mrs W. (meditating), he remains a little standing as though lost in thought, then suddenly emits a single hiccup of such force that he is almost thrown off his feet. Startled from her knitting Mrs D., from her book Miss C., from her stage meditation Mrs W., survey him with indignation. L. remains standing a little longer, absorbed & motionless, then on a wide tack returns cautiously to the door, which he does not close behind him. His unsteady footsteps are heard on the stairs. Between the three women exchange of looks. Gestures of disgust. Mouths opened and shut. Finally they resume their occupations.

Mrs W.   Words fail us.

Mrs D.   Now this is where a writer for the stage would have us speak no doubt.

Mrs W.   He would have us explain Levett.

Mrs D.   To the public.

Mrs W.	The ignorant public.
Mrs D.	To the gallery.
Mrs W.	To the pit.
Miss C.	To the boxes.
Mrs W.	Mr Murphy.
Mrs D.	Mr Kelly.
Miss C.	Mr Goldsmith.
Mrs D.	Let us not speak unkindly of the departed.
Miss C.	The departed?
Mrs D.	Can you be unaware, Miss, that the dear doctor's debt to nature —
Mrs W.	Not a very large one.
Mrs D.	That the dear doctor's debt to nature is discharged these seven years.
Mrs W.	More.
Mrs D.	Seven years to-day, Madam, almost to the hour, neither more nor less.
Miss C.	His debt to nature?
Mrs W.	She means the wretched man is dead.
Miss C.	Dead!
Mrs W.	Dead. D-E-A-D. Expired. Like the late Queen Anne and the Rev. Edward ——.
Miss C.	Well I am heartily sorry indeed to hear that.
Mrs W.	So was I, Miss, heartily sorry indeed to hear it, at the time, being of the opinion, as I still am, that before paying his debt to nature he might have paid his debt to me. Seven shillings and sixpence, extorted on the contemptible security of his *Animated Nature*. He asked for a guinea.
Mrs D.	There are many, Madam, more sorely disappointed,

willing to forget the frailties of a life long since trans-
ported to that undiscovered country from whose —

Mrs W. *(striking the floor with her stick)*. None of your Shakespeare
to me, Madam. The fellow may be in Abraham's
bosom for aught I know or care, I still say he ought to
be in Newgate.

Mrs D. *(sighs and goes back to her knitting)*.

Mrs W. I am dead enough myself, I hope, not to feel any great
respect for those that are so entirely.

Silence.

Mrs W. Also I should very much like to know, Madam, if the
power of speech has not deserted you, for what reason
it is improper in poor Poll here to mention the 'dear
doctor', and proper in you to pronounce the sacred
name of that drunken staymaker Hugh Kelly, dead and
damned these five years.

Mrs D. You are mistaken, Madam.

Mrs W. In what am I mistaken?

Mrs D. In saying that Mr Kelly is no longer with us. It is
impossible that the creator of *False Delicacy* should have
been laid to rest and the fact not come to my notice.

Mrs w. Your notice! After fifty years of dropped stitches, pious
exertions and charity-brats, you still speak of your
notice.

Mrs D. *(scorns to reply)*.

Mrs W. And your 'laid to rest'! Laid to rest in lakes of boiling
small-beer, with his Dublin publican papa, that's
where he's laid to rest, your stayless, playless, briefless,
drunken party-scribbler.

Mrs D. Miss Carmichael, would you have the great goodness to
close the door.

Miss C. I would not, Madam.

Mrs W. *(at the top of her voice)*. KELLY IS DEAD, MADAM.

Mrs D.   *(rising)*. I have nothing more to say, Madam, but that you are mistaken, most offensively mistaken. *(Exit, banging door behind her)*.

Enter Mrs D. She speaks from the threshold.

Mrs D.   Mr Kelly is alive and, I trust, drawing his pension without encumbrance. Mr Kelly may be poorly, but he is alive, and, I pray God, drawing his pension without encumbrance. *(Exit, banging door.)*

Enter Mrs D. as before.

Mrs D.   Should however Mr Kelly, by some extraordinary haphazard, be no longer alive —

Mrs W.   Nor drawing his pension without encumberland.

Mrs D.   And the fact not have come to my notice, I . . . I . . . *(Weeps)*.

Mrs D.   I shall regret it bitterly . . . bitterly . . . *(Exit, closing door softly)*.

Silence.

Mrs W.   Forgive me. I was musing.

Silence.

Mrs W.   I was musing as to whether what she . . . what the . . . *(Breaks off. Strikes floor with stick)*. Pest!

Silence.

Mrs W.   I was musing thus: is what she bitterly regrets, what already it may be she . . . *(Breaks off. Strikes floor with stick)*. PEST!

Silence.

Mrs W.   *(in a strong decided tone)*. What will the woman bitterly regret, if she does not do so already, the death of Kelly or the fact not having come to her notice.

Silence.

Mrs W.   There is a notice of the mind and there is a notice of the heart. The first is nothing. And the heart is cold.

Silence.

Mrs W. *(now evidently talking to herself).* For years, for how many years every day, dead, whose name I had known, whose face I had seen, whose voice I had heard, whose hand I had held, whose — but it is idle to continue. Yesterday, in the flower of her age, Mrs Winterbotham, the greengrocer of the Garden; Monday, Mr Pott of the Fleet; Sunday, in great pain, in his home in Islington, after a lingering illness, surrounded by his family, the Very Reverend William Walter Okey, Litt.D., LL.D; Saturday, at Bath, suddenly, Miss Tout; Friday, — but it is idle to continue. I know —

Miss C. And to-day, Madam?

Mrs W. *(with a start).* I beg your pardon?

Miss C. And to-day, Madam.

Mrs W. To-day is not yet over, Miss Carmichael.

Silence.

Mrs W. I know they are dead, their deaths are come to the notice of my mind.

Silence.

Mrs W. When my father, Mr Zachariah Williams, died, on the 12th of June, seventeen hundred and fifty-five (old time), at twelve at night, in his eighty third year, after an illness of eight months, in full possession of his mental faculties, I knew at once he was dead. He died, and at once I knew he was dead. I wept, because one weeps, when one's father dies. I remember turning, that morning, with tears in my eyes, whose vigour even then was beginning to abate, the pages of his pamphlet: *An Account of an Attempt to Ascertain the Longitude at Sea: with a Table of the Variations at the most Remarkable Cities in Europe.*

Silence.

Mrs W. But it did not come to the notice of my heart until the Christmas following.

Silence.

Miss C. 'Death meets us everywhere, and is procured by every instrument and in all chances, and enters in at many doors; by violence —'

Mrs W. What twaddle is this, Miss Carmichael?

Miss C. I am reading from my book, Madam.

Mrs W. I did not suppose you were inventing it.

Miss C. 'By violence and secret influence; by the aspect of a star and the stink of a mist —'

Mrs W. The stink of a mist?

Miss C. Yes, Madam, the stink of a mist.

Mrs W. Continue, continue.

Miss C. 'Of a mist; by the emissions of a cloud and the meeting of a vapour; by the fall of a chariot and the stumbling at a stone; by a full meal or an empty stomach; by watching at the wine or by watching at prayers; by the sun or the moon; by a heat or a cold; by sleepless nights or sleeping days; by water frozen or water thawed; by a hair or a raisin —'

Mrs W. A hair or a raisin?*

Miss C. Yes, Madam, a hair or a raisin.

Mrs W. How do you suppose death enters in by a hair, Miss Carmichael?

Miss C. Perhaps a horse-hair is meant, Madam.

Mrs W. Perhaps so indeed. I know if death would be content to enter into me by a horse-hair, or by any other manner of hair for that matter, I should be very much obliged to him.

Miss C. 'By a hair or a raisin; by violent exertion or by sitting still; by severity or dissolution; by God's mercy or

*Beckett's fair copy ends here, but the holograph continues to 'Taylor.'

God's anger; by everything in Providence and everything in manners, by everything in nature and everything in chance.'

Silence.

Mrs W.   Brown for a guinea.

Miss Carmichael rises.

Mrs W.   I say: Brown for a guinea.

Miss C.   I hear you, Madam.

Mrs W.   Then answer me. Is it Brown or is it not Brown?

Miss C.   Brown or Black, Madam, it is all one to me.

Mrs W.   Is it possible she reads and does not know what she reads.

Miss C.   I read so little, Madam, it is all one to me.

Mrs W.   Turn to the title page, my child, and tell me is it Brown.

Miss C.   *(turning to the title page).* Taylor.

COME AND GO

Sitting centre side by side stage right to left Flo, Vi and Ru. Very erect, facing front, hands clasped in laps.

Silence

VI

　　When did we three last meet?

RU

　　Let us not speak.

Silence

Exit Vi right

Silence

FLO

　　Ru.

RU

　　Yes.

FLO

　　What do you think of Vi?

RU

I see little change. (*Flo moves to centre seat, whispers in Ru's ear. Appalled.*) Oh! (*They look at each other. Flo puts her finger to her lips.*) Does she not realize?

FLO

God grant not.

Enter Vi. Flo and Ru turn back front, resume pose. Vi sits right

Silence

FLO

Just sit together as we used to, in the playground at Miss Wade's.

RU

On the log.

Silence

Exit Flo left

Silence

RU

Vi.

VI

Yes.

RU

How do you find Flo?

VI

She seems much the same. (*Ru moves to centre seat, whispers in Vi's ear. Appalled.*) Oh! (*They look at each other. Ru puts her finger to her lips.*) Has she not been told?

RU

God forbid.

Enter Flo. Ru and Vi turn back front, resume pose. Flo sits left

Silence

RU

Holding hands . . . that way.

FLO

Dreaming of . . . love.

Silence

Exit Ru right

Silence

VI

Flo.

FLO

Yes.

VI

How do you think Ru is looking?

FLO

One sees little in this light. (*Vi moves to centre seat, whispers in Flo's ear. Appalled.*) Oh! (*They look at each other. Vi puts her finger to her lips.*) Does she not know?

VI

Please God not.

Enter Ru. Vi and Flo turn back front, resume pose. Ru sits right

Silence

VI

May we not speak of the old days? (*Silence.*) Of what came after? (*Silence.*) Shall we hold hands in the old way?

After a moment they join hands as follows: Vi's right hand with Ru's right hand, Vi's left hand with Flo's left hand, Flo's right hand with Ru's left hand, Vi's arms being above Ru's left arm and Flo's right arm. The three pairs of clasped hands rest on the three laps

Silence

FLO

I can feel the rings.

Silence

CURTAIN

Successive positions

1	FLO	VI	RU
2 {	FLO		RU
		FLO	RU
3	VI	FLO	RU
4 {	VI		RU
	VI	RU	
5	VI	RU	FLO
6 {	VI		FLO
		VI	FLO
7	RU	VI	FLO

Hands

Ru   Vi   Flo

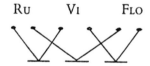

Lighting

Soft, from above only and concentrated on playing area. Rest of stage as dark as possible.

Costume

Full-length coats, buttoned high, dull violet (Ru),
dull red (Vi), dull yellow (Flo). Drab nondescript
hats with enough brim to shade faces. Apart from
colour differentiation three figures as alike as possible. Light shoes with rubber soles. Hands made up
to be as visible as possible. No rings apparent.

Seat

Narrow benchlike seat, without back, just long
enough to accommodate three figures almost touching.
As little visible as possible. It should not be clear
what they are sitting on.

Exits

The figures are not seen to go off stage. They should
disappear a few steps from lit area. If dark not suffi-
cient to allow this, recourse should be had to screens
or drapes as little visible as possible. Exits and
entrances slow, without sound of feet.

Ohs

Three very different sounds.

Voices

As low as compatible with audibility. Colourless
except for three "ohs" and two lines following.

Three Dialogues

I
Tal Coat

B. — Total object, complete with missing parts, instead of partial object. Question of degree.

D. — More. The tyranny of the discreet overthrown. The world a flux of movements partaking of living time, that of effort, creation, liberation, the painting, the painter. The fleeting instant of sensation given back, given forth, with context of the continuum it nourished.

B. — In any case a thrusting towards a more adequate expression of natural experience, as revealed to the vigilant coenaesthesia. Whether achieved through submission or through mastery, the result is a gain in nature.

D. — But that which this painter discovers, orders, transmits, is not in nature. What relation between one of these paintings and a landscape seen at a certain age, a certain season, a certain hour? Are we not on a quite different plane?

B. — By nature I mean here, like the naivest realist, a composite of perceiver and perceived, not a datum, an experience. All I wish to suggest is that the tendency and accomplishment of this painting are fundamentally those of previous painting, straining to enlarge the statement of a compromise.

D. — You neglect the immense difference between the significance of perception for Tal Coat and its significance for the great majority of his predecessors, apprehending as artists with the same utilitarian servility as in a traffic jam and improving the result with a lick of Euclidian geometry. The global perception of Tal Coat is disinterested, committed neither to truth nor to beauty, twin tyrannies of nature. I can see the compromise of past painting, but not that which you deplore in the Matisse of a certain period and in the Tal Coat of today.

B. — I do not deplore. I agree that the Matisse in question, as well as the Franciscan orgies of Tal Coat, have prodigious value, but a value cognate with those already accumulated. What we have to consider in the case of Italian painters is not that they surveyed the world with the eyes of building contractors, a mere means like any other, but that they never stirred from the field of the possible, however much they may have enlarged it. The only thing disturbed by the revolutionaries Matisse and Tal Coat is a certain order on the plane of the feasible.

D. — What other plane can there be for the maker?

B. — Logically none. Yet I speak of an art turning from it in disgust, weary of its puny exploits, weary of pretending to be able, of being able, of doing a little better the same old thing, of going a little further along a dreary road.

D. — And preferring what?

B. — The expression that there is nothing to express, nothing with which to express, nothing from which to express, no power to express, no desire to express, together with the obligation to express.

D. — But that is a violently extreme and personal point of view, of no help to us in the matter of Tal Coat.

B.—

D. — Perhaps that is enough for today.

II
Masson

B. — In search of the difficulty rather than in its clutch. The disquiet of him who lacks an adversary.

D. — That is perhaps why he speaks so often nowadays of painting the void, 'in fear and trembling'. His concern was at one time with the creation of a mythology; then with man, not simply in the universe, but in society; and now . . . 'inner emptiness, the prime condition, according to Chinese esthetics, of the act of painting'. It would thus seem, in effect, that Masson suffers more keenly than any living painter from the need to come to rest, i.e. to establish the data of the problem to be solved, the Problem at last.

B. — Though little familiar with the problems he has set himself in the past and which, by the mere fact of their solubility or for any other reason, have lost for him their legitimacy, I feel their presence not far behind these canvases veiled in consternation, and the scars of a competence that must be most painful to him. Two old maladies that should no doubt be considered separately: the malady of wanting to know what to do and the malady of wanting to be able to do it.

D. — But Masson's declared purpose is now to reduce these maladies, as you call them, to nothing. He aspires to be rid of the servitude of space, that his eye may 'frolic among the focusless fields, tumultuous with incessant creation'. At the same time he demands the rehabilitation of the 'vaporous'. This may seem strange in one more fitted by temperament for fire than for damp. You of course will reply that it is the same thing as before, the same reaching towards succour from without. Opaque or transparent, the object remains sovereign. But how can Masson be expected to paint the void?

B. — He is not. What is the good of passing from one untenable position to another, of seeking justification always on the same plane? Here is an artist who seems literally skewered on the ferocious dilemma of expression. Yet he continues to wriggle. The void he speaks of is perhaps simply the obliteration of an unbearable presence, unbearable because neither to be wooed nor to be stormed. If this anguish of helplessness is never stated as such, on its own merits and for its own sake, though perhaps very occasionally admitted as spice to the 'exploit' it jeopardized, the reason is doubtless, among others, that it seems to contain in itself the impossibility of statement. Again an exquisitely logical attitude. In any case, it is hardly to be confused with the void.

D. — Masson speaks much of transparency — 'openings, circulations, communications, unknown penetrations' — where he may frolic at his ease, in freedom. Without renouncing the objects, loathsome or delicious, that are our daily bread and wine and poison, he seeks to break through their partitions to that continuity of being which is absent from the ordinary experience of living. In this he approaches Matisse (of the first period needless to say) and Tal Coat, but with this notable difference, that Masson has to contend with his own technical gifts, which have the richness, the precision, the density and balance of the high classical manner. Or perhaps I should say rather its spirit, for he has shown himself capable, as occasion required, of great technical variety.

B. — What you say certainly throws light on the dramatic predicament of this artist. Allow me to note his concern with the amenities of ease and freedom. *The stars are undoubtedly superb*, as Freud remarked on reading Kant's cosmological proof of the existence of God. With such preoccupations it seems to me impossible that he should ever do anything different from that which the best, including himself, have done already. It is perhaps an impertinence to suggest that he wishes to. His so extremely intelligent remarks on space breathe the same possessiveness as the notebooks of Leonardo who, when he speaks of *disfazione*, knows that for him not one fragment will be lost. So forgive me if I relapse, as when we spoke of the so different Tal Coat, into my dream of an art unresentful of its insuperable indigence and too proud for the farce of giving and receiving.

D. — Masson himself, having remarked that western perspective is no more than a series of traps for the capture of objects, declares that their possession does not interest him. He congratulates Bonnard for having, in his last works, 'gone beyond possessive space in every shape and form, far from surveys and bounds, to the point where all possession is dissolved.' I agree that there is a long cry from Bonnard to that impoverished painting, 'authentically fruitless, incapable of any image whatsoever', to which you aspire, and towards which too, who knows, unconsciously perhaps, Masson tends. But must we really deplore the painting that admits 'the things and creatures of spring, resplendent with desire and affirmation, ephemeral no doubt, but immortally reiterant', not in order to benefit by them, not in order to enjoy them, but in order that what is tolerable and radiant in the world may continue? Are we really to deplore the painting that is a rallying, among the things of time that pass and hurry us away, towards a time that endures and gives increase?

B. — *(Exit weeping.)*

III
Bram van Velde

B. — Frenchman, fire first.

D. — Speaking of Tal Coat and Masson you invoked an art of a different order, not only from theirs, but from any achieved up to date. Am I right in thinking that you had van Velde in mind when making this sweeping distinction?

B. — Yes. I think he is the first to accept a certain situation and to consent to a certain act.

D. — Would it be too much to ask you to state again, as simply as possible, the situation and act that you conceive to be his?

B. — The situation is that of him who is helpless, cannot act, in the event cannot paint, since he is obliged to paint. The act is of him who, helpless, unable to act, acts, in the event paints, since he is obliged to paint.

D. — Why is he obliged to paint?

B. — I don't know.

D. — Why is he helpless to paint?

B. — Because there is nothing to paint and nothing to paint with.

D. — And the result, you say, is art of a new order?

B. — Among those whom we call great artists, I can think of none whose concern was not predominantly with his expressive possibilities, those of his vehicle, those of humanity. The assumption underlying all painting is that the domain of the maker is the domain of the feasible. The much to express, the little to express, the ability to express much, the ability to express little, merge in the common anxiety to express as much as possible, or as truly as possible, or as finely as possible, to the best of one's ability. What—

D. — One moment. Are you suggesting that the painting of van Velde is inexpressive?

B. — *(A fortnight later)* Yes.

D. — You realize the absurdity of what you advance?

B. — I hope I do.

D. — What you say amounts to this: the form of expression known as painting, since for obscure reasons we are obliged to speak of painting, has had to wait for van Velde to be rid of the misapprehension under which it had laboured so long and so bravely, namely, that its function was to express, by means of paint.

B. — Others have felt that art is not necessarily expression. But the numerous attempts made to make painting independent of its occasion have only succeeded in enlarging its repertory. I suggest that ven Velde is the first whose painting is bereft, rid if you prefer, of occasion in every shape and form, ideal as well as material, and the first whose hands have not been tied by the certitude that expression is an impossible act.

D. — But might it not be suggested, even by one tolerant of this fantastic theory, that the occasion of his painting is his predicament, and that it is expressive of the impossibility to express?

B. — No more ingenious method could be devised for restoring him, safe and sound, to the bosom of Saint Luke. But let us for once, be foolish enough not to turn tail. All have turned wisely tail, before the ultimate penury, back to the mere misery where destitute virtuous mothers may steal stale bread for their starving brats. There is more than a difference of degree between being short, short of the world, short of self, and being without these esteemed commodities. The one is a predicament, the other not.

D. — But you have already spoken of the predicament of van Velde.

B. — I should not have done so.

D. — You prefer the purer view that here at last is a painter who does not paint, does not pretend to paint. Come, come, my dear fellow, make some kind of connected statement and then go away.

B. — Would it not be enough if I simply went away?

D. — No. You have begun. Finish. Begin again and go on until you have finished. Then go away. Try and bear in mind that the subject under discussion is not yourself, not the Sufist Al-Haqq, but a particular Dutchman by name van Velde, hitherto erroneously referred to as an *artiste peintre*.

B. — How would it be if I first said what I am pleased to fancy he is, fancy he does, and then that it is more than likely that he is and does quite otherwise? Would not that be an excellent issue out of all our afflictions? He happy, you happy, I happy, all three bubbling over with happiness.

D. — Do as you please. But get it over.

B. — There are many ways in which the thing I am trying in vain to say may be tried in vain to be said. I have experimented, as you know, both in public and in private, under duress, through faintness of heart, through weakness of mind, with two or three hundred. The pathetic antithesis possession-poverty was perhaps not the most tedious. But we begin to weary of it, do we not? The realization that art has always been bourgeois, thugh it may dull our pain before the achievements of the socially progressive, is finally of scant interest. The analysis of the relation between the artist and his occasion, a relation always regarded as indispensable, does not seem to have been very productive either, the reason being perhaps that it lost its way in disquisitions on the nature of occasion. It is obvious that for the artist obsessed with his expressive vocation, anything and everything is doomed to become occasion, including, as is apparently to some extent the case with Masson, the pursuit of occasion, and the every man his own wife experiments of the spiritual Kandinsky. No painting is more replete than Mondrian's. But if the occasion appears as an unstable term of relation, the artist, who is the other term, is hardly less so, thanks to his warren of modes and attitudes. The objections to this dualist view of the creative process are unconvincing. Two things are established, however precariously: the aliment, from fruits on plates to low mathematics and self-commiseration, and its manner of dispatch. All that should concern us is the acute and increasing anxiety of the relation itself, as though shadowed more and more darkly by a sense of invalidity, of inadequacy, of existence at the expense of all that it excludes, all that it blinds to. The history of painting, here we go again, is the history of its attempts to escape from this sense of failure, by means of more authentic, more ample, less exclusive relations between representer and representee, in a kind of tropism towards a light as to the nature of which the best opinions continue to vary, and with a kind of Pythagorean terror, as though the irrationality of pi were an offence against the deity, not to mention his creature. My case, since I am in the dock, is that van Velde is the first to desist from this estheticized automatism, the first to admit that to be an artist is to fail, as no other dare fail, that failure is his world and the shrink from it desertion, art and craft, good housekeeping, living. No, no, allow me to expire. I know that all that is required now, in order to bring even this horrible matter to an acceptable conclusion, is to make of this submission, this admission, this fidelity to failure, a new occasion, a new term of relation, and of the act which, unable to act, obliged to act, he makes, an expressive act, even if only of itself, of its impossibility, of its obligation. I know that my inability to do so places myself, and perhaps an innocent, in what I think is still called an unenviable situation, familiar to psychiatrists. For what is this coloured plane, that was not there before. I don't know what it is, having never seen anything like it before. It seems to have nothing to do with art, in any case, if my memories of art are correct. *(Prepares to go.)*

D. — Are you not forgetting something?

B. — Surely that is enough?

D. — I understood your number was to have two parts. The first was to consist in your saying what you — er — thought. This I am prepared to believe you have done. The second —

B. — *(Remembering, warmly)* Yes, yes, I am mistaken, I am mistaken.